# Sacred Architecture and Experience

BAPS Shri Swaminarayan Mandir, Robbinsville, New Jersey

Brahmaswarup
Pramukh Swami Maharaj

Guruhari
Mahant Swami Maharaj

BAPS Swaminarayan Sanstha® | www.baps.org/robbinsville

*93-year-old Pramukh Swami Maharaj in front of the mandir on August 8, 2014, two days before the inauguration*

# Dedication

The BAPS Shri Swaminarayan Mandir in Robbinsville, New Jersey is a Hindu place of worship (mandir) dedicated to Bhagwan Swaminarayan. This mandir is the vision of His Holiness Pramukh Swami Maharaj, the fifth guru in the spiritual lineage of Bhagwan Swaminarayan. For years, thousands of BAPS devotees offered their time, energy, and contributions in the fulfillment of that vision, and on Sunday, August 10, 2014, Pramukh Swami Maharaj enshrined the sacred images and opened the mandir to all.

This book is dedicated to Pramukh Swami Maharaj, the mandir's creator, and the many thousands of his devotees, young and old, who served selflessly to make their guru's vision a reality.

*Volunteers putting finishing touches on the mandir in the days leading up to the inauguration.*

## Bhumi Pujan
*July 21, 2009 – Bochasan, India*

*Pramukh Swami Maharaj performs the soil sanctification ceremony in Bochasan using soil from the newly acquired land in Robbinsville, New Jersey. This sacred soil was later used to sanctify the construction site in Robbinsville.*

## Reviewing Plans
*September 6, 2010 – Sarangpur, India*

*Pramukh Swami Maharaj offers guidance on the mandir's plans to Ishwarcharan Swami and his team of swamis responsible for the mandir's construction.*

## Shilanyas Pujan
*July 12, 2010 – Delhi, India*

*Pramukh Swami Maharaj sanctifies the foundation stones that would later be ritually placed in the scripturally prescribed areas of the mandir foundation.*

# Creation

From conception to completion, Pramukh Swami Maharaj created the mandir in five years and gifted it to the current and future generations of the Northeastern United States.

## Concrete Pouring
*April 19, 2011*

*After the foundation stone-laying ceremony, a massive raft foundation was poured that would support the immense weight of the marble mandir.*

## Murti Pratistha
*August 10, 2014 – Robbinsville, NJ*

*Pramukh Swami Maharaj installing the sacred images of Bhagwan Swaminarayan and Gunatitanand Swami (Akshar Purushottam Maharaj).*

## Exterior Mandovar
*October 6, 2012*

*The carved marble exterior wall of the mandir was then erected with a shear wall support.*

## Pillars
*April 13, 2013*

*Ninety-eight pillars were assembled as the primary load-bearing elements of the mandir.*

## Exterior Facade
*April 12, 2014*

*After the mandir was completed, the structure of the Pramukh Swami Mandapam was erected surrounding the mandir.*

3

BAPS Shri Swaminarayan Mandir, Robbinsville, NJ on a winter evening

# Welcome

The mandir welcomes people of all backgrounds to explore and appreciate the Hindu devotional traditions that have brought peace and happiness to countless lives. This book follows a visitor's path through the mandir, introducing readers to the sacred architecture and divine experience of the BAPS Shri Swaminarayan Mandir in Robbinsville, New Jersey.

# MAYUR DWAR

## Peacock Gate

---

MAYUR DWAR

---

DWARPALS

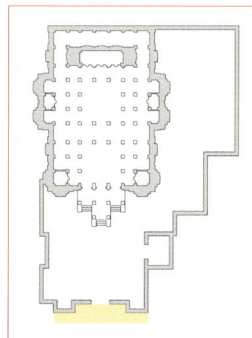

# Mayur Dwar

"Mayur" means peacock and "Dwar" means gate. Visitors enter the mandir by passing through the Mayur Dwar, named for the hundreds of peacocks carved into this 50-foot-tall limestone gate. Peacocks play an important role in Hindu culture and are celebrated for their beauty and grace. The intricately-carved Mayur Dwar is part of the ancient tradition of exquisite entrances in Hindu mandirs that mark a devotee's departure from the temporal world of conflict and confusion and their entry into a divine realm of peace and spiritual bliss.

*Eight of the 270 peacocks that make up the Mayur Dwar*

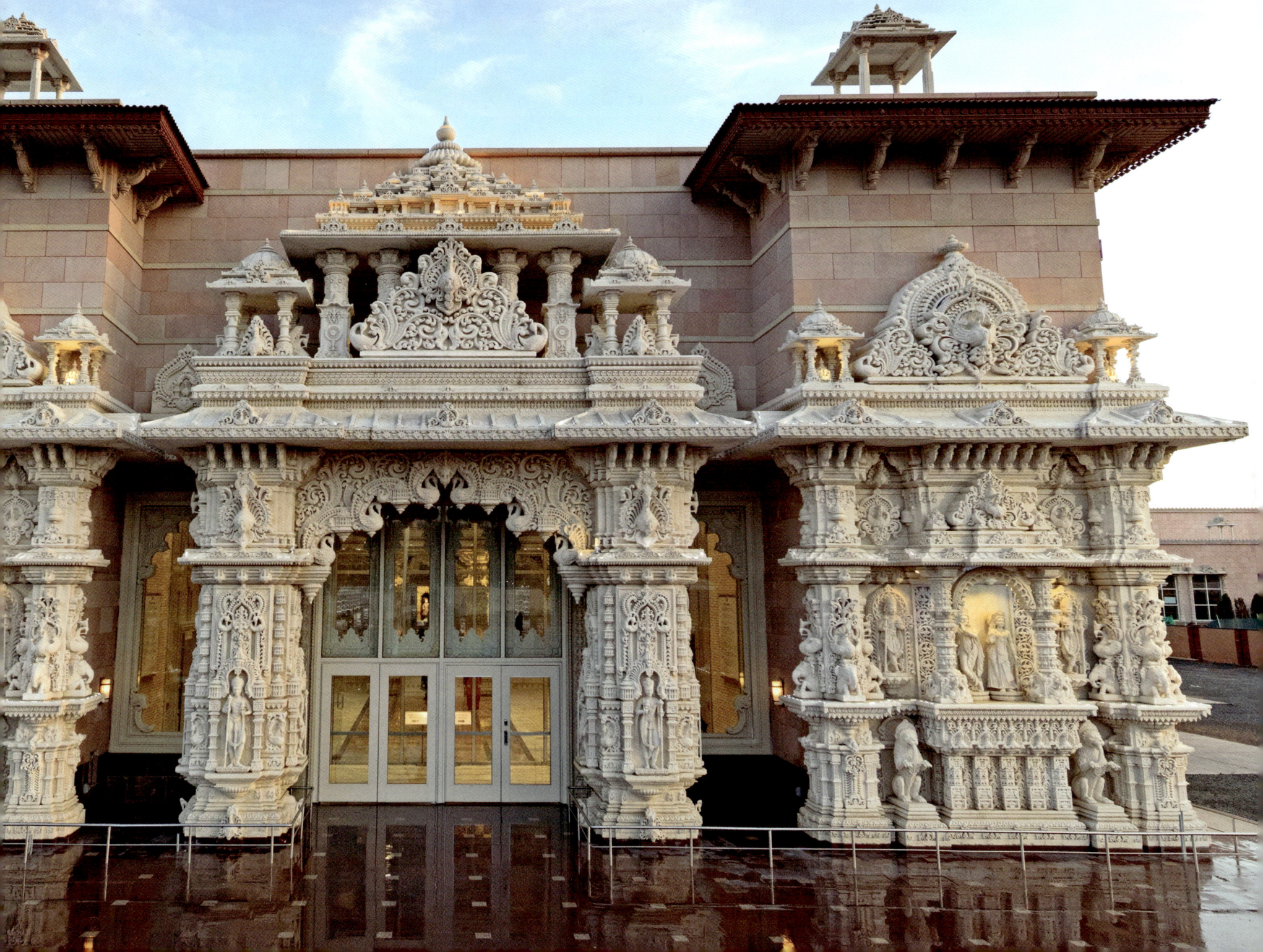

*A pair of dwarpals flanking Akshar Purushottam Maharaj in the Mayur Dwar*

*A pair of dwarpals flanking Shri Radha-Krishna in the Mayur Dwar*

# Dwarpals

The dwarpals, or door guards, are usually placed in pairs at the mandir entrances and doorways. They hold a staff and stand guard in the devoted service of the mandir's presiding deity. The dwarpals remind the devotee that before entering the sacred premises of the mandir, which is the abode of God, all worldly thoughts should be left outside. Since God also resides in one's heart, the dwarpals also remind the devotee to vigilantly stand guard at the gateway of one's own consciousness to prevent worldly thoughts and desires from penetrating into one's heart.

# THE MANDIR

**A Hindu Place of Worship**

---

MANDIR

---

MANDIR CONSTRUCTION

---

ANCIENT DEVOTIONAL ARCHITECTURE

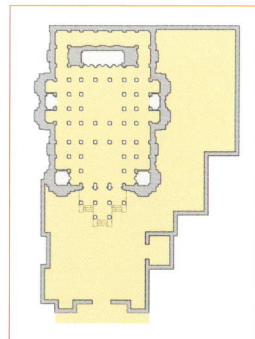

# Mandir

A mandir is a Hindu place of worship. Hindus visit the mandir to seek the blessings of God and guru. God's divine presence in the mandir graces worshipers with peace and inspires them to attain greater spiritual heights.

*A worshiper turning the mala while chanting God's name and doing darshan*

*Aerial view of Shri Swaminarayan Mandir, Robbinsville under construction in January 2014*

# Mandir Construction

This mandir is made of marble that was quarried in Italy and shipped to India, where thousands of traditional artisans carefully carved each piece. Then, these pieces were shipped to New Jersey and assembled into the mandir. The mandir took four years to complete and it was inaugurated on August 10, 2014 by Pramukh Swami Maharaj.

*Skilled artisans carefully install a carved lotus in one of the mandir's ceilings*

# Ancient Devotional Architecture

Over millennia, mandirs have evolved into masterpieces of devotional architecture. Their design principles were preserved through the ages in ancient treatises on sacred Hindu art and architecture called the sthapatya shastras. The wealth of spiritual and cultural meaning embedded in the architectural directives of the sthapatya shastras have been carved into the various elements of this mandir.

In addition to its carvings, the mandir is also architecturally remarkable for a structural design that uses ancient engineering principles to calculate the size and orientation of the pillars and beams to support the immense weight of the stone. Many ancient mandirs built according to these design principles have survived the ravages of time for millennia. So, it is no exaggeration to say that this mandir is designed to last for more than a thousand years.

# ROOP CHOKI

## Entry Portico

---

WELCOME

---

BHAGWAN SWAMINARAYAN

---

SPIRITUAL PURIFICATION

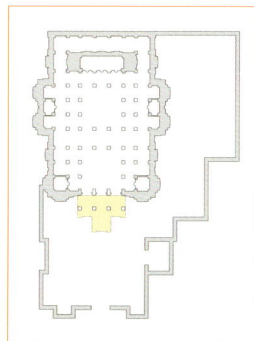

## Welcome

These two pillars in the mandir's entry portico include carvings of liberated souls singing, playing instruments, and holding flowers. Each of these poses represents a traditional form of greeting. Since guests are revered in Hinduism, visitors will see many such representations of welcome throughout the mandir.

# Bhagwan Swaminarayan

An image of Bhagwan Swaminarayan, to whom this mandir is dedicated, is carved on the ceiling of the entry portico. He offers his blessings while surrounded by liberated souls who welcome visitors.

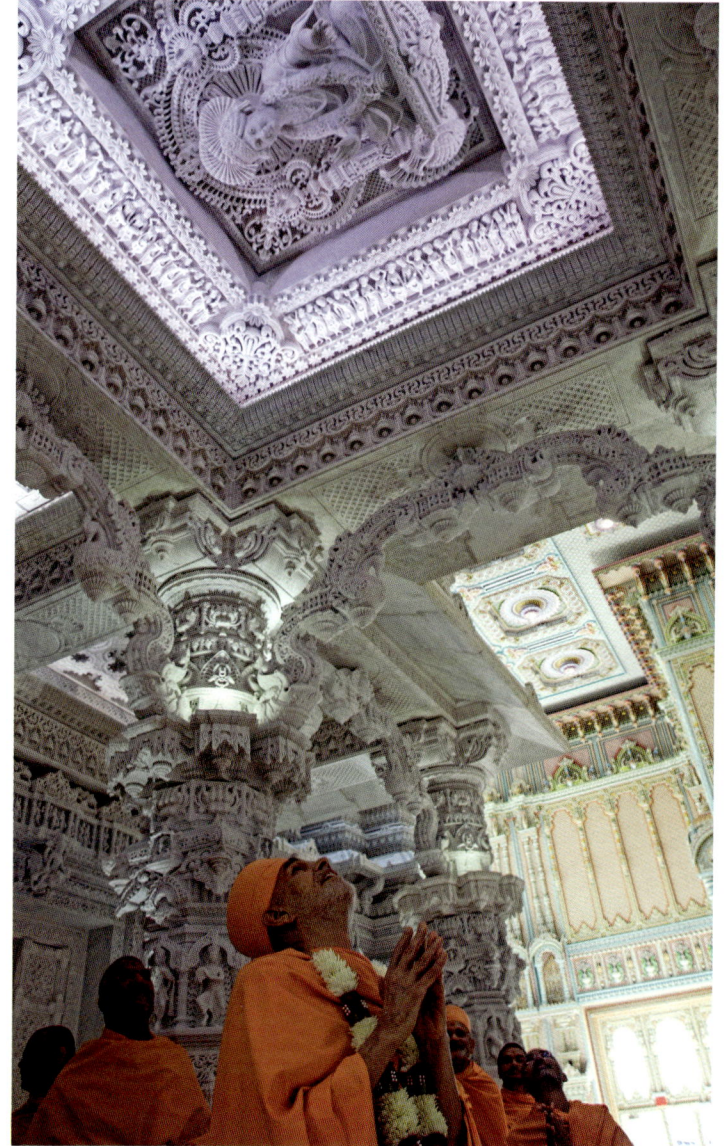

*Mahant Swami Maharaj, the guru of the BAPS Swaminarayan Sanstha, bows to the image of Bhagwan Swaminarayan upon entering the mandir*

## *Spiritual Purification*

The pillars on both sides of the entry portico have representations of some of the holy rivers of India as the goddesses Ganga, Yamuna, Saraswati, and Narmada. The holy waters of these rivers are considered to be physically and spiritually purifying. Thus, as devotees walk past these pillars into the mandir, they symbolically prepare to leave behind the mundane world and spiritually purify themselves as they make their way towards the Divine.

*The goddess form of the holy Ganga River*

# DWARSHAKH

## Door Frame

---

DWARSHAKH

---

CARVINGS

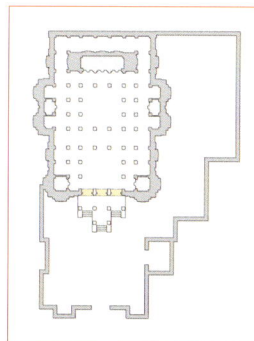

# Dwarshakh

The dwarshakh, or door frame, is comprised of two vertical jambs supporting the horizontal lintel. The lintel contains a central dedicatory block, in this case, an image of Ganesh in the central door frame and images of Vishnu on the side door frames. Throughout the dwarshakh are carvings of deva pairs, including Sita-Ram, Shiv-Parvati, Lakshmi-Narayan and Brahma-Saraswati, which emphasize the important Hindu principle of the devotee's personal relationship with God.

# Carvings

Hidden amongst the carvings of vines in the dwarshakh are many different animals, including peacocks, elephants, lions, monkeys, deer, rabbits, goats, parrots, cows, and squirrels. Such carvings of animals throughout the mandir remind us that Hinduism emphasizes being in harmony with nature.

Throughout the mandir, there are carvings of liberated souls, devas, ancient sages, and exemplary devotees who are both objects of reverence and sources of spiritual inspiration. There are also various depictions of classical dance and music, both elements of the Hindu tradition of loving devotion to God. Additionally, images of auspicious animals, birds, flowers, and items used in daily worship have been integrated into the mandir's artistic carvings. This variety of carvings serve to indicate that mandirs are visual models of the totality of creation, representing the cosmos and everything in it.

# DOMES

---

MAJESTIC DOMES

———

GESTURES OF WELCOME

———

FLOOR ART

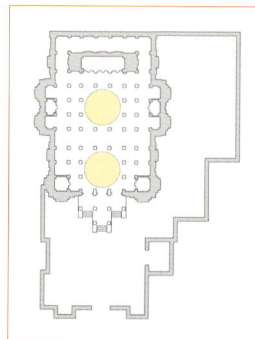

# Majestic Domes

The soaring spaces underneath the 34-foot high, 30-foot diameter domes provide a sense of majesty that complements the intricacy of the mandir's carvings.

The domes are not single pieces of stone, but rather composites of different interlocking stone slabs. In the middle of the dome, there is a beautiful marble centerpiece. Like a keystone, this single piece locks all the stone pieces used to keep the large dome in place.

*Expert artisans installing the dome key*

*View upwards capturing both of the mandir's intricately carved domes*

*View of Akshar Purushottam Maharaj
from the center of the first dome*

## Gestures of Welcome

Both domes are replete with carvings of flowers, peacocks, elephants, devas, liberated souls, and celestial beings playing instruments. Around the top of the dome are numerous liberated souls offering garlands and sixteen large figures of liberated souls showering flowers in a gesture of joyous welcome to all who visit the mandir.

# Floor Art

The pristine white marble floors of the mandir are punctuated by a variety of inlaid stone designs, the most spectacular of which are the two large stone "medallions", or circular design patterns, directly below the two domes. In this type of traditional Indian stone art, called *parchin kari*, each stone is selected for its naturally occurring hue and carefully pieced together to form a variety of exquisite patterns. Along with various auspicious design elements such as lotuses, bells, and floral patterns, the first medallion is designed with an elephant motif, while the second medallion has a peacock motif. Both the elephant and peacock are considered auspicious animals in Hinduism.

# CEILINGS, ARCHES & PILLARS

CEILINGS

ARCHES

PILLAR COMPONENTS

ATTENTION TO DETAIL

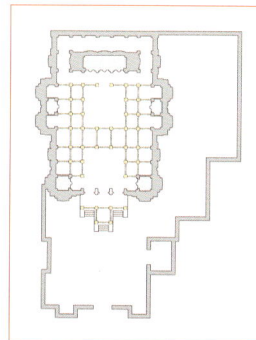

# Ceilings

In addition to the two large domes, the mandir has fifty-eight intricately carved ceilings of stunning symmetry, with the sacred lotus as the primary design element. The ceilings also display carved conch shells, bells, and other auspicious ritual implements.

# Arches

The arch between two pillars is called a toran. It is used as both an architectural element, helping to distribute the immense weight of the stone structures above, and also as an ornamental feature, adding a distinctive elegance to the straight lines of the mandir's post and lintel construction. The arches in the mandir are distinctive for their carvings of peacocks in addition to the typical floral motif.

# Pillar Components

## Shirsha

The top of the pillar is the shirsha, or capital.

## Stambh

The middle section of the pillar is called the stambh. The stambhs in the mandir include carvings of peacocks, bells, liberated souls, images of Ganesh with musical instruments, and great sages and devotees of Hinduism.

## Kumbhi

The kumbhi, or base of the pillar, contains carvings of various devas, such as Lakshmi or Saraswati, or liberated souls of Akshardham in a variety of stylized poses.

## *Attention to Detail*

The profusion of intricate carvings on every available surface engenders a sense of other-worldly divinity in anyone who enters the mandir. But behind the smallest detail of each carving is an immense labor of love.

For example, to fully sculpt just a single pillar would require four expert artisans sixty days. Looking at the ninety-eight such pillars throughout the mandir, along with the countless other carved elements, one gets a sense of the amount of time and dedication it took to create the mandir.

पूजा दोडिया

Punja Dodia

*Inspirational devotees and sages memorialized on the pillars*

# INSPIRATIONAL ICONOGRAPHY

Spiritual luminaries of the Hindu past have been enshrined upon the pillars of the mandir both to commemorate their important contributions to the richness of Hindu thought and practice and to inspire and guide visitors to live spiritually-elevated lives. The pillars surrounding the first dome commemorate the spiritual luminaries of ancient and medieval Hinduism. They include inspiring personalities from the Ramayan, like Lakshman, Bharat, and Shabri; from the Shrimad Bhagavat, like Janak, Dhruv, and Prahlad; and from the Mahabharat, like Arjun. The pillars surrounding the second dome commemorate the great swamis and devotees of Bhagwan Swaminarayan's era, including Muktanand Swami, Gopalanand Swami, Kushalkuvarba, and Dada Khachar. The lives of these great personalities inspire visitors to cultivate universal values such as honesty, empathy, non-violence, equanimity, perseverance, devotion to God, service, purity, integrity, forgiveness, and transcendence. In this section, some of these great personalities have been highlighted.

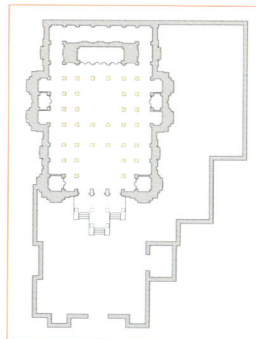

# Meerabai

Meerabai was a 15th-century saint-poet who was revered for her profound devotion to Shri Krishna. After her marriage to the prince of Chittorgarh in Rajasthan, the royal family attempted to restrict her devotional activities. However, she continued visiting temples, listening to discourses from holy sadhus, and composing and singing devotional hymns to Shri Krishna. Eventually, she renounced the life of the royal palace and adopted the life of a pilgrim, traveling to spots sanctified by Shri Krishna and expressing her intense love for him through her devotional hymns. She composed hundreds of hymns, many of which are still sung today. She is depicted here with her royal ornaments covered by the simple garb of an ordinary pilgrim, holding the dotara (stringed instrument) and kartals (cymbals) as she sings hymns with her eyes almost closed in the ecstasy of devotion to God.

# Gargi

Gargi was one of the great sages of the Vedic era. Renowned for her sharp intellect and knowledge of the Vedas, she remained immersed in scriptural study and debates about Brahman. She was most famous for a debate with the great Sage Yagnavalkya in the royal court of King Janak. Through her incisive questions in that debate, which is recorded in the Upanishads, she and Yagnavalkya discussed the all-pervasive Aksharbrahman, which supports the cosmos, as well as the supreme Parabrahman, or God, the highest, ultimate reality.

# Prahlad

Prahlad was a great child devotee of Vishnu. His father, the evil Hiranyakashipu, ruled all three worlds and considered Vishnu his enemy. However, when Prahlad was in the womb, he had heard the sermons of the great sage and devotee of Vishnu, Narad. Thus, from a young age, he worshiped Vishnu and chanted his name, infuriating his father. Because he would not stop, Hiranyakashipu attempted to murder him on multiple occasions, but Vishnu Bhagwan protected him, and Prahlad never gave up chanting Vishnu's name. Finally, Vishnu incarnated as Nrusinh and killed Hiranyakashipu, protecting his steadfast child-devotee.

# Janak

King Janak, the ruler of Mithila, was celebrated for his great wisdom and spiritual realization. Although he was a king, he remained detached from worldly pleasures and immersed in devotion to God. He understood the transient nature of worldly objects and thus was not attracted to them. Once, he was listening to spiritual discourses in an assembly of great sages. A great sage created an illusion that Mithila was on fire. While the rest of the assembly ran to secure their valuables, King Janak continued serenely listening to the discourses. When the great sage asked why he, too, did not run from the discourse to secure his valuables, King Janak replied, "While the city may be burning, nothing of mine is on fire." He remains an example of a life of deep spiritual wisdom coupled with the exercise of worldly responsibilities.

# Muktanand Swami

Muktanand Swami was a senior monk of Bhagwan Swaminarayan who is revered for his profound saintliness. He embodied countless saintly virtues, including compassion, love, devotion, immense self-discipline, and great humility. He was an exceptional poet and composed many hymns. He was also a great scholar and one of the compilers of Bhagwan Swaminarayan's discourses into the scripture, the Vachanamrut. In Muktanand Swami's final years, at Bhagwan Swaminarayan's behest, he contributed to the sacred literature of the Sampradaya by writing sacred texts recounting incidents of Bhagwan Swaminarayan's life. Thus, he is depicted here holding the pages of a manuscript indicating his dedication to fulfilling Bhagwan Swaminarayan's command.

# Kushalkuvarba

Kushalkuvarba, the 19th-century queen mother of the kingdom of Dharampur, exemplifies how absolute faith in the manifest form of God inspires loving devotion to him. From the first time Kushalkuvarba heard of Bhagwan Swaminarayan's glory, she yearned to meet him. At her invitation, Bhagwan Swaminarayan graced her kingdom together with his sadhus and devotees, and Kushalkuvarba served everyone with loving devotion. When it was time for Bhagwan Swaminarayan to leave, she offered her entire kingdom to him, but he refused it.

In his discourses recorded in the Vachanamrut, Bhagwan Swaminarayan remembers his visit to Dharampur, describing Kushalkuvarba as a model for doing darshan and imbibing the divine image of God into one's heart. Here she is depicted offering a basket of flowers indicating her invitation to Bhagwan Swaminarayan to grace her kingdom and memorializing her faith that contact with the manifest form of God is necessary for ultimate liberation.

# AUSPICIOUS ICONOGRAPHY

At first glance, the mandir carvings may appear to be a froth of fractal forms, but a closer look reveals an array of stylized and realistic representations of auspicious Hindu symbols. Profound cultural and spiritual meanings have been embedded within these auspicious Hindu symbols from antiquity. This section will clarify the meanings of some of the auspicious symbolic motifs that are found throughout the mandir.

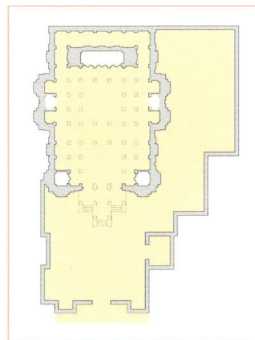

# Peacocks

Peacocks are celebrated in Hinduism for their beauty, dignity, and grace. They also symbolize purity and divinity due to their close association with many devas and avatars, serving as vehicles for Kartikeya and Saraswati, while their feathers are part Shri Krishna's crown. The peacock is one of the most popular symbols in the mandir, found everywhere from the outside gate to the flooring, arches, walls, and pillars.

# Tilak-Chandlo

A tilak is a religious symbol applied on the forehead by many Hindus. Followers of Bhagwan Swaminarayan apply a variation of the tilak, called the tilak–chandlo. The saffron, U-shaped tilak represents God, and the round, red chandlo in the center of the tilak represents the ideal devotee. So, this mark symbolizes a devotee remaining forever in the service of God, reflecting the eternal Hindu principle of devotion to God and his ideal devotee. Throughout the mandir, one sees this motif reinforcing the centrality of service to God in a devotee's life.

# Bells

The ringing of bells is considered auspicious in Hinduism, and thus is a part of worship rituals like arti and puja. The sound of the bell represents the sacred syllable, Om. The body of the bell represents Ananta (god of time), the tongue symbolizes Saraswati (goddess of speech), and the handle or chain signifies the energy of the prana (vital breath). The sound of the bell is believed to awaken the power of mantras chanted during the worship rituals. The ringing sound facilitates the senses and mind to focus on God, as it drowns away other noises.

# Purna Kumbh

The purna kumbh is an auspicious pot that is a symbol of perfection, goodness, and prosperity. During the churning of the ocean by the devas and demons, Bhagwan emerged bearing a purna kumbh containing immortalizing nectar. Brahma, Shiva, Vishnu, and Devi are believed to reside in the purna kumbh's mouth, neck, bottom, and middle, respectively. Thus, the purna kumbh is an important element in many sacred Hindu rituals. Stylized purna kumbhs with lotus flowers, stalks, leaves, and other auspicious symbols are sculpted on pillars and pinnacles of Hindu mandirs.

# Conch Shells

The conch shell symbolizes the sacred syllable Om, dharma, victory, and auspiciousness. The sonorous sound of the conch is made to honor and please God. It is also a victory call of good over evil. The sound of the conch inspires one's mind toward an attitude of prayer.

# Akshar Deri

The Akshar Deri is a memorial shrine to Gunatitanand Swami, built 150 years ago on the site of his final rites in Gondal, Gujarat. The Akshar Deri is one of the most sacred places of pilgrimage for Swaminarayan devotees because Gunatitanand Swami is the ideal devotee and personal manifestation of Akshardham, the divine abode of Bhagwan Swaminarayan. Thus, the Akshar Deri motif around the mandir symbolizes ideal devotion, selfless sacrifice, indomitable faith, and supreme spiritual enlightenment. The shape surrounding the peacock in the above photo is a representation of the Akshar Deri.

## Elephants

Elephants have always been honored in India for their strength, grace, and kindness. Hindu scriptures and folklore have portrayed the elephant in nature as strong and fearless, intelligent and emotional, gentle and caring. They have also celebrated the loving relationship of elephants with humans and the Divine. For centuries, elephants have been essential to the construction of mandirs, helping carry logs and large blocks of stone. Thus, elephants are often honored in mandir architecture not just as design elements, but as an entire plinth, where they steadily carry the mandir on their backs in service of God.

## Lotus

The lotus symbolizes truth, auspiciousness, and beauty, which are essential virtues of God. In fact, many parts of God's divine body are described using the metaphor of a lotus: his lotus eyes, his lotus feet, his lotus hands, etc. The lotus, though born out of and rooted in mud, blossoms unaffected by it. The mud represents the material world, and the ability to remain unaffected by it symbolizes transcendence. So, a lotus symbolizes a person of enlightenment, untainted by the mire of baser instincts. Alternatively, the stylized lotus petals around the base of the mandir suggest that while the mandir has emerged from the material world, it rests on a massive lotus, and so remains transcendent and unaffected by the material world due to God's presence.

# Variety of Lotuses

Throughout the mandir, one finds such depictions of the lotus in realistic and stylized forms. Some of the various representations of lotuses found on the ceilings, pillars, walls, domes, and arches of the mandir are shown here.

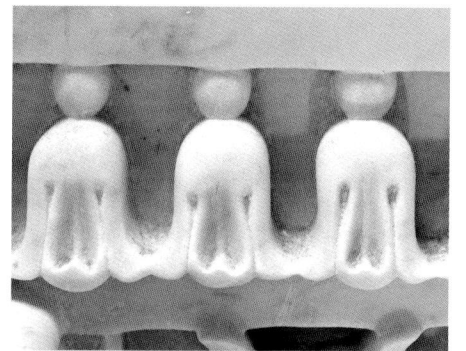

# GARBHA GRUH

## Inner Sanctum

---

MURTI PUJA

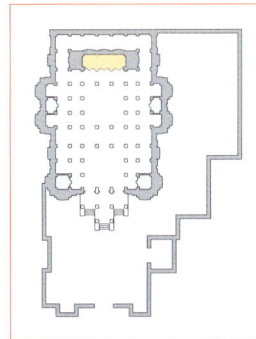

*The arti ceremony being performed before the murtis in the garbha gruh*

# Murti Puja

Murti puja, or the worship of God manifest in sacred images, is central to the practice of Hinduism. Murti puja allows devotees to physically express their devotion, and it fuses faith into daily practice. Devotees care for and offer service to the murtis understanding them to be the manifest form of the deities. In the mandir, the deities reside in the garbha gruh, or inner sanctum. Every morning, the deities are adorned with colorful clothes and ornaments in what is called the shangar, or ornamenting ritual. In addition, murtis are offered meals and afternoon rest. The arti ritual, in which sacred lamps are ritually waved before the murtis while hymns are sung of their glory, occurs five times a day. These physical forms of devotion foster a loving relationship between the devotee and God.

*A swami performing the arti ritual of Akshar Purushottam Maharaj*

*Swamis engrossed in daily prayers*

# DEITIES

---

SHRI AKSHAR PURUSHOTTAM MAHARAJ

(BHAGWAN SWAMINARAYAN & GUNATITANAND SWAMI)

---

SHRI GHANSHYAM MAHARAJ

---

SHRI HARIKRISHNA MAHARAJ & SHRI RADHA KRISHNA

---

SHRI SHIV PARVATI PARIVAR

---

SHRI RAM SITA PARIVAR

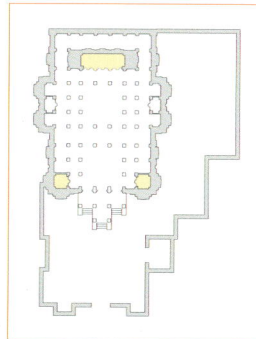

# Shri Akshar Purushottam Maharaj
# (Bhagwan Swaminarayan & Gunatitanand Swami)

Bhagwan Swaminarayan (1781–1830) incarnated in northern India to reveal profound spiritual truths through his teachings, correct misguided religious practices, and grant eternal liberation to countless souls. He established the Swaminarayan Sampradaya at the age of 20 and inspired a spiritual renaissance, introducing social reforms, serving the poor and needy, and preaching against superstitions, addictions, and violence. He initiated 3,000 swamis and was worshiped as God during his lifetime by countless individuals. To continue his work of moral and spiritual regeneration, he promised to remain ever-present on earth through an unbroken succession of enlightened gurus.

Gunatitanand Swami (1784–1867) was the first spiritual successor of Bhagwan Swaminarayan. He was an ideal swami, singularly devoted to God, dedicated to the service of others, and constantly engaged in sharing his profound spiritual wisdom. He was revealed by Bhagwan Swaminarayan to be Akshar (or Aksharbrahman), the eternally perfect devotee, and the closest entity to God as extolled in the Vedas, Upanishads, and Bhagavad Gita. As Akshar, Gunatitanand Swami remains manifest on earth as the enlightened guru, guiding spiritual aspirants towards eternal liberation.

When the murtis of Bhagwan Swaminarayan (Purushottam) and Gunatitanand Swami (Akshar) are installed together, they are known as Akshar Purushottam Maharaj. They reflect the highest philosophy of ultimate liberation in which one must become like Akshar, the ideal devotee, to remain eternally in the loving service of Purushottam (God).

## Shri Ghanshyam Maharaj

Bhagwan Swaminarayan was known by the name of Ghanshyam in his childhood. Ghanshyam renounced home at the age of eleven to embark on a seven-year, 8,000-mile spiritual journey across the length and breadth of India. Walking alone, barefoot, and with almost no possessions, he sanctified places of pilgrimage and inspired thousands to lead a life rooted in morality and spirituality. Ending his journey in the state of Gujarat, he built six majestic mandirs and inspired the creation of scores of scriptural texts by swamis of the fellowship. Bhagwan Swaminarayan's spiritual teachings were recorded in the Vachanamrut—a collection of his discourses encapsulating Vedic wisdom and methods for implementing it in daily life.

# Shri Harikrishna Maharaj & Shri Radha Krishna

This shrine houses a murti of another childhood form of Bhagwan Swaminarayan, known as Harikrishna Maharaj (on the left), made of metal alloy.

In the center is the murti of Shri Krishna, who incarnated on the earth approximately 5,000 years ago. One of the most well-known scriptures of Hinduism is the Bhagavad Gita, which contains Shri Krishna's spiritual teachings.

On Shri Krishna's right is Radha, his ideal devotee, who exemplifies unflinching love and absolute devotion to God.

# *Shri Shiv Parvati Parivar*

Shri Shiva, also worshiped as Maheshwar, Shambhu, Shankar, Rudra, and by other names, enacts the destroyer aspect of the universe. Shiva, a profound yogi, is adorned with symbols of simplicity and asceticism.

Shri Parvati is the eternal consort and perfect devotee of Shiva. She is also known as Uma, Durga, Shakti, and by many other names. Like Parvati, devotees desire to attain a deep, loving bond with God.

Shri Ganesh is revered as the deva of auspiciousness. He is honored at the beginning of Hindu rituals as the granter of good fortune, remover of obstacles, and bestower of wisdom. He is known by many names, including Ganapati, Vinayaka, and others. He is also the devout son of Parvati.

Shri Kartikeya, also known as Murugan, Subramanya, Skanda, and by other names, is the captain of the devas and son of Shiva-Parvati. In the struggle against evil, his valor and power are unique and redemptive.

# Shri Ram Sita Parivar

Shri Ram, an avatar of Vishnu, is popularly known as Maryada Purushottam—a noble observer of all the religious ideals. His life, chronicled in the sacred scripture, the Ramayan, teaches us to strive for truth, justice, determination, compassion, and family harmony.

Shri Sita is his eternal consort. Sita's perfect devotion towards Ram exemplifies unconditional love, fidelity, positivity, and unparalleled faith. Her relationship with Shri Ram inspires devotees to attain the same level of devotion towards God.

Shri Lakshman, the brother of Ram, is an ideal celibate who demonstrated how to dedicate one's life in the selfless service of God.

Shri Hanuman, a devotee of Ram, is revered as a protector against evil forces. He epitomized the virtues of obedience, inner strength, loyalty, wisdom, and humility. Hence, he is revered by all spiritual aspirants as 'ideal service personified'.

# LINEAGE OF GURUS

BHAGATJI MAHARAJ

SHASTRIJI MAHARAJ

YOGIJI MAHARAJ

PRAMUKH SWAMI MAHARAJ

MAHANT SWAMI MAHARAJ

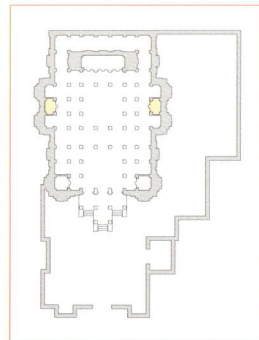

# Bhagatji Maharaj

Bhagatji Maharaj (1829-1897) was the second spiritual successor of Bhagwan Swaminarayan. Often shunned and insulted by the ignorant, his intense desire to worship God endeared him to many. He lived a life of tremendous spiritual endeavor and unfailing faith in following the wishes of his guru, Gunatitanand Swami. His ideal moral and spiritual enlightenment singled him out as the successor to Gunatitanand Swami even though he was not ordained as a swami.

# Shastriji Maharaj

Shastriji Maharaj (1865-1951) was the third spiritual successor of Bhagwan Swaminarayan. Shastriji Maharaj was a profound scholar of Sanskrit and the Hindu scriptures and a powerful orator. He was responsible for elucidating the importance of the worship of Akshar and Purushottam, or Bhagwan Swaminarayan along with his ideal devotee, Gunatitanand Swami, which is the foundational theology of the Swaminarayan Sampradaya. Dynamic and resolute, Shastriji Maharaj overcame insurmountable obstacles to build five grand mandirs, consecrating within them the sacred images of Gunatitanand Swami (Akshar) and Bhagwan Swaminarayan (Purushottam). In 1907, he formally established the Bochasanwasi Shri Akshar Purushottam Swaminarayan Sanstha (BAPS).

## Yogiji Maharaj

Yogiji Maharaj (1892–1971) was the fourth spiritual successor of Bhagwan Swaminarayan. His life was one of selfless service, inspiring sermons, and the sharing of profound spiritual love. He initiated children's and youth activities within BAPS, promoting personal spirituality and service to society. He inspired spiritual activities beyond India, helping Hindus in England, America, and parts of Africa to preserve their faith and values.

## Pramukh Swami Maharaj

Pramukh Swami Maharaj (1921–2016) was the fifth spiritual successor of Bhagwan Swaminarayan. This mandir is the fruit of his vision and blessings, and it was consecrated by him on August 10, 2014.

Under his leadership, BAPS grew into an international Hindu spiritual and humanitarian organization with over 3,300 centers worldwide. He dedicated his life to the well-being of others, traveling throughout the world to foster love, peace, harmony, righteousness, faith in God, and service to humanity. With genuine care and compassion, he reached out to all members of society. He was recognized and respected among Hinduism's greatest spiritual teachers. His credo was: "In the joy of others, lies our own.

# Mahant Swami Maharaj

Mahant Swami Maharaj (b. 1933) is the sixth and current spiritual successor of Bhagwan Swaminarayan. He was ordained a swami by Yogiji Maharaj in 1961 and named Sadhu Keshavjivandas. Due to his appointment as the head (mahant) of the mandir in Mumbai, he became known as Mahant Swami. His devout, humble, and service-focused life earned him the innermost blessings of Yogiji Maharaj and Pramukh Swami Maharaj. Mahant Swami Maharaj travels throughout the world, inspiring people through his insightful discourses to progress on the spiritual path. His virtuous lifestyle and profound devotion to Bhagwan Swaminarayan and his gurus are ideals toward which devotees strive.

# GARBHA GRUH MANDOVAR

## Wall Surrounding the Inner Sanctum

———————

ELEPHANTS

———

DEITIES

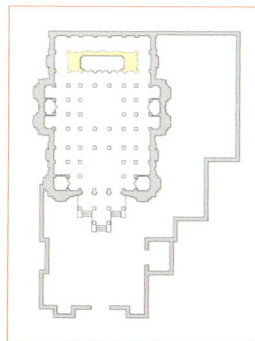

*The wall behind the mandir's central shrine, or garbha gruh*

Pramukh Swami Maharaj blessed the murtis of this mandir on July 22, 2012, in Ahmedabad, India. A depiction of that ceremony is carved into the wall behind the inner sanctum to commemorate that historic event. The murtis were then brought to the United States and installed in the mandir by Pramukh Swami Maharaj on August 10, 2014.

## Elephants

Along the outer wall of the inner sanctum, carvings of elephants greet God by playing various instruments and offering flowers and other worship implements. The backs of the elephants all display intricate and individualized ornamented tapestries. Not a single one is alike. Elephants are commemorated in the carvings of Hindu mandirs because they were previously the main vehicles used to haul stones to the mandir construction site. Their service is forever memorialized in stone and inspires devotees to selflessly serve God.

# Deities

Other deities and avatars of God and their ideal devotees such as Lakshmi-Narayan, Nar-Narayan, Vithoba-Rukmini, and Balaji-Padmavati grace the outer wall of the inner sanctum.

*Shri Nar-Narayan*

*Shri Balaji-Padmavati*

*Shri Lakshmi–Narayan*

*Shri Vithoba–Rukmini*

# MURALS OF IDEAL DEVOTION

WORSHIPING GOD WITH HIS IDEAL DEVOTEE

GOD INCARNATES WITH HIS IDEAL DEVOTEE

PROMISE TO REMAIN EVER-PRESENT

GUNATITANAND SWAMI'S INITIATION

INSPIRING IDEAL DEVOTION

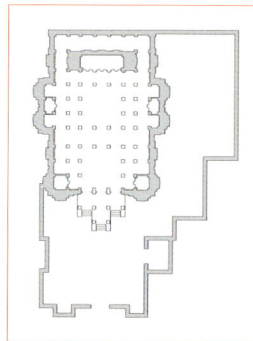

*In this stone mural, Bhagwan Swaminarayan reveals himself to be Purushottam and Gunatitanand Swami to be Akshar during the spring festival in Sarangpur*

# *Worshiping God with His Ideal Devotee*

In accordance with Hinduism's ancient teachings of venerating and serving God together with his ideal devotee, Rama is worshiped with Sita, Krishna with Radha, and Shiva with Parvati. In this same spiritual tradition, Purushottam is worshiped together with Akshar.

Akshar and Purushottam are supreme, divine entities whose limitless glory has been sung by the Vedas and the Upanishads.

Purushottam, also known as Parabrahman or Paramatma, is supreme, omnipotent, and eternally possesses a divine personal form.

Akshar, or Aksharbrahman, is the ideal devotee of the supreme being and connects individual souls with Purushottam.

Purushottam manifested on earth as Bhagwan Swaminarayan, and Akshar manifested on earth as Gunatitanand Swami.

This mandir is dedicated to the eternal pair of Akshar and Purushottam, Gunatitanand Swami and Bhagwan Swaminarayan, who are installed in the main shrine.

A series of stone murals honor the worship of God and his ideal devotee, Bhagwan Swaminarayan and Aksharbrahman Gunatitanand Swami, by depicting selected historical interactions showing the divine devotional bond between them.

# God Incarnates with His Ideal Devotee

To show the path of liberation and the highest spiritual ideals to all spiritual seekers, Bhagwan Swaminarayan (1781–1830) manifested on earth from Akshardham with his ideal devotee, Aksharbrahman Gunatitanand Swami (1784–1867).

## Promise to Remain Ever-Present

In 1830, Bhagwan Swaminarayan departed from this earth at the age of 49. The next day, noticing some blades of grass near a stream, Gunatitanand Swami thought, "Just as its source of life is water, Bhagwan Swaminarayan was my life, and he has departed." With this thought, he fainted. Bhagwan Swaminarayan appeared in a divine form, lifted him up, and said, "I have not gone. I reside eternally in you."

## Gunatitanand Swami's Initiation

Bhagwan Swaminarayan ordained 25-year-old Mulji Sharma into the sadhu order, named him Gunatitanand Swami, and said, "Today, I am extremely delighted to have initiated the manifest form of my Akshardham, Aksharbrahman Mulji Sharma. As Gunatitanand Swami, he will become famous throughout the world." The date of this historic event was January 20, 1810.

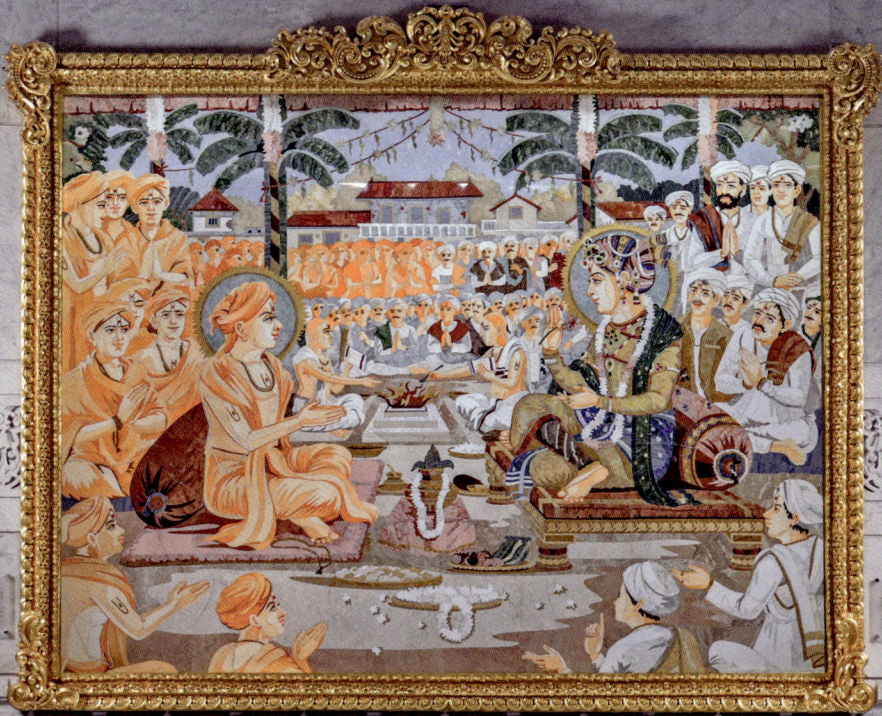

## *Inspiring Ideal Devotion*

Radha's perfect devotion to Krishna and Sita's perfect devotion to Rama inspires spiritual aspirants to become ideal devotees and offer perfect devotion to God. Similarly, Bhagwan Swaminarayan taught devotees to become brahmarup (spiritually ideal) through the association of God's ideal devotee, Akshar, and offer ideal devotion to Purushottam.

Bhagwan Swaminarayan also taught that Purushottam remains forever present on this earth through a perfect Guru, who is the manifest form of Aksharbrahman. Only through association with such an Aksharbrahman Guru can one attain ultimate liberation and remain in the eternal service of Purushottam. This is the significance of worshiping Akshar along with Purushottam, or the ideal devotee along with God.

*A stone mural of Gunatitanand Swami devotionally swinging Bhagwan Swaminarayan while other swamis and devotees sing hymns*

# MANDOVAR

## Outer Wall

———————————

MANDOVAR

———

DEVOTIONAL RITUALS

———

GANESH

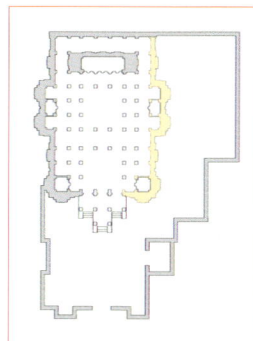

# Mandovar

The mandir's outer wall is called a mandovar. Along with its architectural elements, such as stylized balconies and windows, the mandovar is distinctive for its iconographic elements which emphasize joyous devotion to God.

# Devotional Rituals

The relationship between God and devotee is a central motif in this mandir. The outer wall of the mandir contains various carvings displaying a devotee's offerings of devotion to God. For example, devotees are seen doing arti, offering a garland, and offering food to God. In Hinduism, the fabric of daily devotional rituals weaves the presence of God into devotees' everyday lives by serving as regular reminders of God's infinite glory and grace.

## Ganesh

Around the mandovar are 48 unique images of a four-armed dancing Ganesh. Each Ganesh is sculpted in different poses with different symbolic items in each hand.

# PRAMUKH SWAMI MANDAPAM

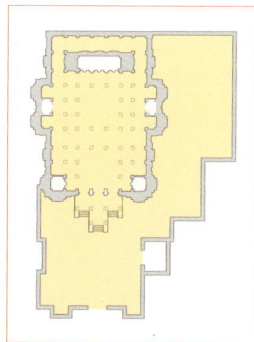

# Pramukh Swami Mandapam

The building that encloses the mandir is called the Pramukh Swami Mandapam in honor of the mandir's creator. Its pastel hues compliment the white marble mandir, providing an overall effect that is aesthetically stunning. Essential quotations from important Hindu scriptures adorn the walls of the Pramukh Swami Mandapam to guide, inspire, and enlighten visitors.

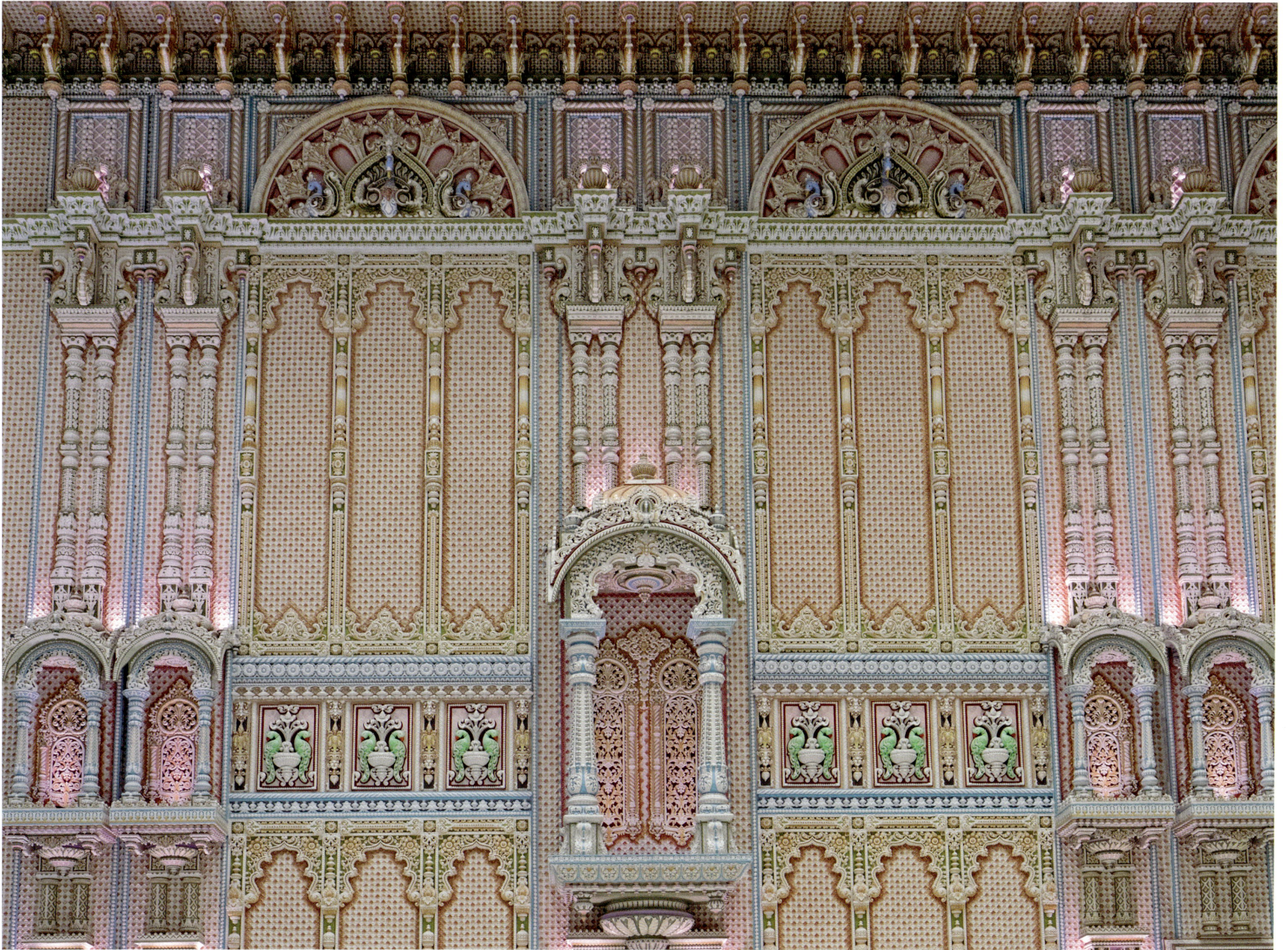

# ABHISHEK MANDAPAM

---

## GHANSHYAM MAHARAJ ABHISHEK MURTI

---

## ABHISHEK CEREMONY

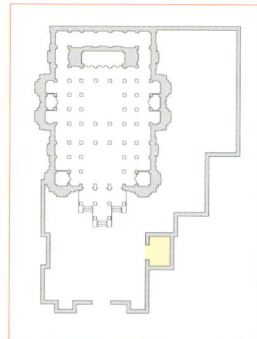

# Ghanshyam Maharaj Abhishek Murti

Bhagwan Swaminarayan, known in his childhood as Ghanshyam, was born on April 3, 1781 in the village of Chhapaiya in northern India. On September 28, 1784, three-year-old Ghanshyam was playing with his friends on the outskirts of Chhapaiya when he climbed into the branches of a pipal tree and sat gazing towards the setting sun. His friends inquired, "What are you looking at?" Ghanshyam revealed, "Many spiritual seekers have taken birth in the West; I want to go to the West for them." As his young friends looked on mutely, how could they know that Ghanshyam would one day travel to western India to liberate countless souls, and that his spiritual teachings would continue to spread to the furthest corners of the Western world?

At the age of 11, Ghanshyam left home, assumed the name Nilkanth, and walked barefoot on an 8,000-mile, 7-year pilgrimage around India. He settled in the western Indian region of Gujarat where his divine charisma earned him a place in the hearts of millions as Bhagwan Swaminarayan.

His Holiness Mahant Swami Maharaj installed this abhishek murti of Ghanshyam Maharaj and gave his blessings that everyone's prayers would be fulfilled here.

## Abhishek Ceremony

An abhishek is a special Hindu ritual rooted in faith and devotion seeking God's grace. Performed by gently pouring water over the murti, it is an offering, an expression of reverence, and a prayer for spiritual progress, peace, and fulfillment of one's aspirations.

# Satsang—A Spiritual Community

The mandir is not just a beautiful monument to an ancient faith tradition; it is the focal point of a living, vibrant spiritual community and a catalyst for individual spiritual awakening. The mandir is a center for Satsang—a congregation focused on devotion, spirituality, service, and moral living with the aim to realize the ultimate truths about God, guru, and the soul. Thus, an essential component of the mandir is its assembly hall and classrooms, which host weekly spiritual discourses by learned swamis, weekly classes for all ages, and religious festivals throughout the year.

*A learned swami teaches about sacred wisdom from holy Hindu scriptures*

*A girl accepts the sanctified flame of the arti ritual during a Children's Diwali Celebration*

*Boys sit in the weekly bal sabha, or Hinduism classes for children*

*Devotees attend a weekly spiritual discourse in the mandir's main assembly hall*

# Swaminarayan Akshardham

Swaminarayan Akshardham, the Mahamandir currently under construction, will eventually become the focal point of this complex. Akshardham is the name of the divine abode of God. The Swaminarayan Akshardham Mahamandir aims to offer a glimpse of the inexpressible majesty and beauty of this divine abode on earth.

The Swaminarayan Akshardham Mahamandir will soar over 150 feet high and be encircled by a pink sandstone colonnade called a parikrama. Architecturally uplifting, the exquisite Hindu art and architecture of Swaminarayan Akshardham will invite visitors to explore the timeless spirituality and traditions embedded within it. As a vibrant center of the profound culture and wisdom of Hinduism, Akshardham aims to be a place to celebrate traditions, encourage learning, foster faith, and kindle a spiritual lifestyle that grants peace, fulfillment, and happiness.

The construction site was blessed by His Holiness Pramukh Swami Maharaj in August 2014 and Mahant Swami Maharaj in September 2017. Upon its completion, Swaminarayan Akshardham will be a humble tribute to Bhagwan Swaminarayan, the Aksharbrahman gurus, avatars, devas, and great sages of Hinduism.

Through the fall foliage, in a winter blizzard, on a quiet spring dawn or dusk, or in a mid-summer thunderstorm, through every season of the year and in every season of our life, the BAPS Shri Swaminarayan Mandir in Robbinsville, New Jersey remains a sanctuary of spiritual serenity that fosters faith and celebrates our invaluable religious heritage.